CELEBRATIONS
T H A T
MATTER

CELEBRATIONS
T H A T
MATTER

A Year-round Guide to
Making Holidays Meaningful

HARRIETT DILLER

AUGSBURG • MINNEAPOLIS

CELEBRATIONS THAT MATTER
A Year-round Guide to Making Holidays Meaningful

Scripture quotations unless otherwise noted are from the Holy Bible: New International Version. Copyright © 1978 New York International Bible Society. Used by permission of Zondervan Bible Publishers.

Cover design: Connie Helgeson-Moen
Interior art: RKB Studios, Inc.

Library of Congress Cataloging-in-Publication Data

Diller, Harriett, 1953–
   Celebrations that matter : a year-round guide to making holidays
meaningful / Harriett Diller.
     p.   cm.
   ISBN 0-8066-2498-1
   1. Holidays—United States.   2. United States—Religious life and
customs.   3. United States—Social life and customs.   I. Title.
   GT4803.D55   1990
   394.2'0973—dc20   90-1175
                                         CIP

The paper used in this publication meets the minimum requirements of American National Standard for Information Sciences—Permanence of Paper for Printed Library Materials, ANSI Z329.48-1984. ∞ ™

Manufactured in the U.S.A.   AF 9-2498

94   93   92   91   2   3   4   5   6   7   8   9   10

CONTENTS

PREFACE

People have always needed holidays. Holidays provide a break from routine. They give us something to look forward to. They are a time of light and love, of gifts and good food. They are a time of rest and refreshment.

Or are they?

Some would offer an alternative view of holidays. "I'd do away with them," one person told me. "A birthday's just like any other day," another person said. And who hasn't heard someone say about a holiday, "It's too commercialized"?

The way we have celebrated has changed over time. It used to be that the church was the biggest influence on holidays. Now the business world seems to have taken control. Instead of the church calendar determining the beginning of the Christmas season, the shopping calendar does. Christmas displays and Santa Claus appear in stores long before Thanksgiving. And as soon as Christmas is over, the stores shove aside Christmas displays and move in Valentine's Day items. Businesses have even snatched birthday celebrations out of the home and moved them into fast-food restaurants.

Such trends suggest that people aren't far wrong in suggesting that holidays have lost their true meanings.

But we don't have to let these trends dictate how we will celebrate our holidays. *Celebrations That Matter* offers suggestions that will aid you in replacing unsatisfactory celebrations with meaningful traditions.

In this day when often both parents work outside the home and families spend less time together than ever before, traditions are critical to the well-being of families. Yet most people's main complaint about holidays is the extra stress that they bring on lives already too busy. People resort to store-bought versions of holidays because they desperately need to save time. This book will help you celebrate holidays without spending a lot of time you don't have. It is designed to bring meaning back into holiday celebrations.

Though geared primarily to home settings, the ideas in this book may be used successfully in other settings— at church, in classrooms, with groups—wherever and however you gather to celebrate. Have a year's worth of fun!

ONE

NEW YEAR

Ringing in the New Year in a More Christian Way

There's nothing at all Christian about the popular notion of celebrating the new year with a hard-drinking party on New Year's Eve followed by a hangover on New Year's Day. Fortunately, many people are beginning to frown on this type of celebration, thanks in part to nationwide campaigns against drinking and driving. The trend toward partying at hotels in order to avoid drinking and driving is a step toward a safer New Year's celebration. But there are still better ways to celebrate. We can keep New Year's at home. We can celebrate together as families in positive ways. Consider some of the following ideas to bring in the new year:

◆ Play games together on New Year's Eve. Usually, someone in the family has received a new game for Christmas.

♦ Look through your photo albums together. New Year's Eve is a good time to look at photos of your family and paste in those pictures that never made it into the album. Remember past times together.

♦ If you have home videos of the family, show them. Make New Year's Eve a night at the family movies, complete with popcorn.

♦ Let the children stay up later than usual on New Year's Eve and do something special together. Make cookies or bake a cake in honor of the new year.

♦ At the stroke of midnight, gather together to pray for God's continuing grace for the coming year and give thanks for the blessings received in the past year.

♦ Have a candlelight breakfast at midnight on New Year's Eve and talk about your hopes for the new year. Pray together for peace in the world.

♦ In many parts of Africa, it is customary for families to walk outdoors on New Year's Eve and watch the sun set on the old year. Take a walk together and share your thoughts on the passing of the old year and the birth of a new one.

♦ On New Year's Eve, write thank-you notes to family and friends.

♦ If you have snow, hold a snow sculpture festival on New Year's Day. Have each person make snow sculptures relating to the holiday season. For instance:

NEW YEAR

a clock striking midnight	the date of the new year
an hour glass	a candle
Father Time	the New Year's baby

♦ Adopt the old European custom of making a pilgrimage on New Year's Day. Visit friends or relatives. Or, make a phone-call pilgrimage to faraway family.

♦ New Year's is a good time for taking stock of ourselves. Revive the old custom of getting rid of things you don't like about yourself. Write the character traits you would like to get rid of on pieces of paper and make a ritual of throwing them into a fire. Those of us without fireplaces will have to be less dramatic. Pass a small box around the dinner table and have each person drop his or her papers into the box. Seal the box and toss it into the trash.

♦ Send New Year's Day cards instead of Christmas cards. New Year's is a good time to update faraway friends and family on what your family has been doing the past year. By writing cards on New Year's, you can eliminate one activity that causes stress before Christmas. Those receiving cards after Christmas will have more time to read them, too.

♦ At mealtime on New Year's Day, share your wishes for the New Year. Have everyone in the family do as the children in Belgium do. Write New Year's greetings on brightly colored paper and give them to other family members. Or, exchange small gifts.

◆ Go Wassailing on New Year's Day. Though often associated with Christmas, this English custom has its roots in New Year's tradition. People go from house to house, singing songs and offering God's blessings for the New Year. Traditionally, the singers are then invited to drink from a wassail cup, but you might take along a treat to share with the household instead. The word *wassail* comes from an old Saxon greeting, "Waes Hael!" which means "Good health!"

As you go from house to house, carry a wassail branch, an evergreen bough tied to a long stick. Decorate it as you would your Christmas tree. (You might even cut the branch from your tree if you plan to take it down soon.) Traditionally, the wassail branch had red bows tied to it. Consider making one for each person.

◆ Have your own "bowl" game on New Year's Day by playing a game of touch football.

◆ Attend a New Year's service, if your church has one. Make one of your family's resolutions to have daily devotions together.

◆ Resolve to help others in particular ways in the coming year. You might plan to donate food to a local food pantry or choose one charity to support financially as a group this year. Consider projects that involve personal action, like donating time to a service agency or your church.

◆ Resolve to turn old, used items into new, useful items by becoming dedicated recyclers of paper, plastic, cardboard, glass, clothing, and household goods. Consult the Yellow Pages for recycling centers near you.

♦ Adopt the oriental custom of writing poems that express your wishes for the new year. Post everybody's poems around the house as New Year's decorations.

♦ Mark on your calendar all the holidays you plan to celebrate during the new year. Include all the birthdays you intend to commemorate. Resolve to include at least a few holidays you haven't celebrated before.

TWO

VALENTINE'S DAY & ST. PATRICK'S DAY

Celebrating Two Saints' Days

Valentine's Day

According to tradition, St. Valentine was a priest who had his head cut off because of his Christian beliefs. Some say that Valentine fell in love with his jailer's daughter and wrote her letters, thus originating the valentine. Valentine's Day commemorates friendship and love. We can find better ways of celebrating than by going to the nearest discount store and buying lots of candy and a bag of valentines. Valentine's Day is a good day to stress the message of Christian love. It's an appropriate time to look past the commercialism and get back to the basics. Try the following ways to celebrate Valentine's Day this year.

♦ Make homemade valentines using red construction paper and white paper doilies and exchange them with family members at breakfast or dinner on Valentine's Day. For fun, hide little valentine messages around the house and let family members search for them.

♦ Remember people who may not receive valentine greetings. Contact the chaplain at a local correctional facility to get the names of prisoners and send them valentines.

♦ Deliver valentines to people who are homebound or living in nursing homes. Send greetings to people who are hospitalized.

♦ Avoid buying expensive valentine candy by making a Valentine's Day cake instead. Or, make cranberry bread from a box mix. Another alternative is to make red finger gelatin in the shape of little hearts (cut with a cookie cutter).

♦ If you can't celebrate Valentine's Day without chocolate, try this quick recipe:

No-cook fudge
2 sticks margarine
4 heaping teaspoons cocoa
1 pound confectioner's (powdered) sugar
1 cup crunchy peanut butter
1 teaspoon vanilla
Melt butter and mix with peanut butter. Add sugar and cocoa. Pat into a greased pan. Cut into squares or use a heart-shaped cookie cutter. Refrigerate.

♦ Make Valentine's Day toast at breakfast. With a cookie cutter, cut a heart shape into the middle of a slice of bread. Heat margarine in a frying pan. Put the bread in the pan. Break an egg into the heart-shaped hole and cook the egg and bread together.

♦ Use a cookie cutter to make heart-shaped sandwiches for your children's school lunches. Tuck a valentine message or a Bible verse about love in their lunch boxes.

♦ Have a special supper on Valentine's Day. Cut heart-shaped placemats from red and white construction paper. Decorate the table with valentine cards and red balloons. Include a heart-shaped pizza as part of the menu, and for dessert, serve strawberry or cherry ice cream and heart-shaped cookies you've made together with your children.

♦ Make cupcakes together and decorate using the little candies with sayings on them. Share them with neighbors and friends.

♦ Cut hearts out of red construction paper and display them in your windows during the week before Valentine's Day. Decorate a heart-shaped wreath from a craft store and hang it on your front door.

♦ Send a note of appreciation to someone who has done something nice for you. Leave a valentine treat for the person who delivers your paper or mail. Don't forget to thank teachers, bus drivers, daycare providers, and others on whom you depend each day.

♦   Bring back the old custom of decorating a valentine box and filling it with the names of good people throughout the ages. Have each family member draw a name from the box. Each person then strives throughout the coming year to be like the person whose name he or she picked.

♦   Give "love in action" valentines. Write a promise to do something for someone else. You might write "I promise to wash the dishes for a week" or "I promise to read you an extra story tonight" or some other promise on a paper heart and exchange with family members.

♦   Compose and deliver singing valentines to neighbors and friends. Choose familiar tunes like "London Bridge" or "Row, Row, Row Your Boat" and create new lyrics expressing your love for these important people in your lives.

St. Patrick's Day

We celebrate St. Patrick's Day on the date of St. Patrick's death in A.D. 493. St. Patrick was a priest and later a bishop, who was sent to Ireland to convert the Druids to Christianity. He risked death by daring to spread the gospel.

It was St. Patrick who first used the three-leaved shamrock to represent the Trinity of Father, Son, and Holy Spirit. According to popular legend, St. Patrick drove the snakes from Ireland by beating a drum. St. Patrick's Day can be an occasion to honor bravery and devotion like St. Patrick's.

17

◆ Remembering that St. Patrick was a missionary, write letters to missionaries of the church and let them know how much you appreciate their work. Pray for their continuing work in spreading the gospel.

◆ Use this occasion to explore the heritage of the Irish people. The night before St. Patrick's Day, read aloud from a library book about Ireland. Listen to a recording of Irish music. Look up in an encyclopedia the article on Ireland. Locate Ireland on a map of the world.

◆ Make a dinner featuring foods from Ireland. Some possibilities include corned beef and cabbage, potatoes, and meat pie.

◆ In honor of the Irish poetic tradition, learn poems and recite them on St. Patrick's Day.

◆ Have an all-green meal on St. Patrick's Day. Serve green gelatin salad, green beans, pistachio pudding—anything green! At mealtime, discuss St. Patrick's bravery. Ask family members if there are any other people who they think ought to have a day named in their honor.

◆ Make a cake in the shape of a shamrock and ice it with green frosting in honor of St. Patrick. Invite someone you know who may be lonely to share the cake with you.

◆ Cut shamrocks out of green construction paper and display them in your windows during the week preceding St. Patrick's Day.

♦ Hold your own St. Patrick's Day parade. Have everyone come dressed in green or dress as St. Patrick.

♦ According to St. Patrick's *Confession*, he comforted himself with prayer after being sold as a slave. On St. Patrick's Day, discuss ways we are in bondage in our own lives. Pray to God for guidance in finding our way out of this bondage.

♦ Talk about ways we can show courage and energy for God's work as St. Patrick did.

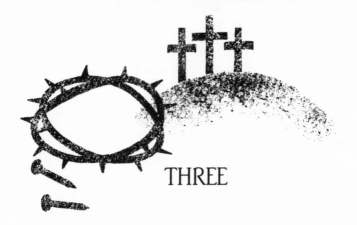

THREE

THE DAYS OF LENT

More Than Mardi Gras

Lent is the period of 40 days, excluding Sundays, beginning with Ash Wednesday and ending with the day before Easter. It is traditionally a time of fasting, self-denial, and devotion among Christians as we commemorate Christ's 40 days in the wilderness and prepare for Easter. Lent is a quiet time for meditation on the meaning of Christ in our lives.

The Lenten season is traditionally preceded by several days of merriment and partying. In various parts of the world, this pre-Lent festival is called Carnival or "fasching" or Mardi Gras. The festive time ends the day before Ash Wednesday—Shrove Tuesday. *Shrove* is a middle English word meaning confession, reminding us that Shrove Tuesday was originally a day for confessing one's sins before the beginning of Lent.

Shrove Tuesday or Fat Tuesday was the traditional time for using up the last bit of fat before Lent. In our

20

time, people still celebrate by eating pancakes, *fas-nachts*, or doughnuts on Shrove Tuesday, but most ignore the 40 days of fasting which are supposed to follow. Do observe Shrove Tuesday, but consider also marking the Lenten season with some sort of fast.

Shrove Tuesday

♦ Start Shrove Tuesday with a pancake breakfast for the family. Discuss the tradition behind eating pancakes on Shrove Tuesday. This was the day to use up the last bits of leftover fat, dairy products, eggs, and meat in the house before Lent began. This would be a good time to discuss your plans for fasting during the Lenten season. Fasting doesn't have to mean going without food entirely. You might choose to eliminate a specific food, like red meat, on one or more days of the week. Use the money you would have spent on that food item for charitable purposes.

♦ Buy *fasnachts* or doughnuts and pack in children's lunch boxes on Shrove Tuesday. Or, make your own quick doughnuts by using canned biscuits available in the refrigerated section of the supermarket. Cut holes in the biscuits and fry them in oil. Roll in granulated or powdered sugar.

♦ Plan a Shrove Tuesday celebration for your family. Fix a special dinner. After dinner, play board games or do something active like ice skating, sledding, or bowling.

♦ In many countries, including some parts of our own country such as New Orleans, the days preceding Lent are a time for dressing up, wearing masks, and partying. Plan a pre-Lent costume party. Ask everyone to get together costumes using only materials they already have at home. Serve doughnuts for refreshments.

Lent

♦ On Ash Wednesday, attend an imposition of the ashes service, where ashes are rubbed in the shape of a cross on one's forehead. This visible symbol reminds us of both death and renewal. Ash Wednesday is a solemn day of repentance.

♦ Make pretzels during Lent. Pretzels were first made by Christians in the Roman empire. Since they did not eat eggs, dairy products, or fat during Lent, they made a dough of flour, salt, and water. They shaped the dough to resemble two arms crossed in prayer to remind them of the prayerful attitude they should take during Lent.

You can make pretzels easily and quickly by using a can of soft bread sticks dough from the refrigerated section of the grocery store. Stretch and twist the dough into pretzel shapes. Bake according to directions. The result tastes more like bread than a pretzel.

♦ Use the Lenten season as a time to try some meatless recipes.

◆ During Lent have daily devotions when you gather together for breakfast or dinner. This is a good practice to continue throughout the year!

◆ Check your local library for books about how other cultures celebrate Lent. Read them aloud during your family time together.

◆ Make a Lenten calendar to collect money for your church.

5¢ for every towel you own. ①	1¢ for every book in your house. ②	5¢ for every pot in your kitchen. ③	10¢ for every book you read this week. ④	10¢ for every chair in your living room ⑤	1¢ for every pair of socks you own. ⑥	10¢ for every newspaper you get. ⑦
25¢ for every hat you own. ⑧	1¢ for every necktie in your house. ⑨	25¢ for every meal you ate out this week. ⑩	10¢ for every hour you watched T.V. yesterday. ⑪	25¢ for everytime you missed church this month ⑫	10¢ for every VCR tape you own. ⑬	25¢ for every T.V. you own. ⑭
25¢ for every VCR you own. ⑮	1¢ for every window in your house. ⑯	5¢ for every cup of coffee today. ⑰	25¢ if you own a dishwasher. ⑱	25¢ if you turned up the heat today. ⑲	1¢ for every picture on your walls. ⑳	10¢ for every phone call you made today. ㉑
25¢ for every time you went to the DR. this month ㉒	10¢ for every time you ate today. ㉓	5¢ for every time you drove a car today ㉔	25¢ for every movie you've seen this month ㉕	5¢ for every audio tape you own. ㉖	5¢ for every blanket you own. ㉗	25¢ for every bathroom in your house. ㉘

Holy Week

Holy Week, the last week before Easter, begins with Palm Sunday. It is traditionally the time when we recall the final days in the life of Jesus. One way people observe Holy Week is by attending church services on Maundy Thursday, Good Friday, and Holy Saturday.

On Maundy Thursday we remember the last supper Jesus shared with his disciples. Good Friday brings to mind his suffering and death on the cross. Easter vigils are held on Holy Saturday so that people may greet the joyous day of resurrection as the hour of midnight strikes. It's appropriate to celebrate Holy Week in special ways. It is a good time to prepare our hearts and homes for Easter.

♦ Follow the Latin American custom of using palm leaves to decorate a cross for Palm Sunday. You can buy palm leaves at a florist shop during the days before Palm Sunday.

To make a palm cross, first cut two 11" x 2" strips of cardboard. Staple a palm leaf to the end of one piece of cardboard, then wrap it around the cardboard as far as it will go. Fasten the leaf by stapling, then wrap another leaf around the cardboard in the same manner. Repeat this process with the second piece of cardboard. When both strips are wrapped with palm leaves, fasten them together into a cross shape, either by stapling or wrapping with twine.

Display your cross during Holy Week. On Easter Sunday, decorate it with flowers.

24

♦ On Palm Sunday, make peace cakes. This could be any sort of cake cut into small pieces. According to an old English custom, people eat the peace cakes together and forget their disagreements.

♦ On Palm Sunday, make posters of Holy Week symbols and display them around the house or in your windows during Holy Week. Possible symbols include:
> The palm branch, to remind us of Jesus' triumphal entry into Jerusalem.
> The basin and pitcher, to remind us that Jesus washed the disciples' feet at the last supper.
> The communion cup and loaf of bread to remind us of the Last Supper.
> The cross to remind us of Jesus' death.
> The crown of thorns to remind us of Jesus' suffering.

♦ Ask everyone in your family or group to draw pictures illustrating events in the life of Jesus. Display these during Holy Week.

♦ Decorate a dead branch with crosses as a symbol of Jesus' crucifixion and our redemption through him. Use a variety of cross designs. Check your church library for a book of symbols of the church that might include a number of cross designs.

♦ Have the whole family pitch in to help with spring cleaning during Holy Week. While cleaning, set aside items to donate to charitable organizations. Or, hold a yard sale and give the proceeds to your church.

◆ Write an Easter letter updating faraway family members and friends on your family's activities and offering your wishes for the Easter season.

◆ During Holy Week, look at art inspired by the life of Jesus either in a museum or an art book from the library.

◆ On Maundy Thursday, honor the tradition of service which goes back to the first Maundy Thursday and gives us our name for the day. "Maundy" refers to the mandate Christ gave his disciples to serve others as he served them by washing their feet. Fill small baskets with useful items such as toothpaste, hand lotion, shampoo, and soap and deliver them to people who are homebound.

◆ Join Christians in many parts of the world by putting candles in your windows during Holy Week.

◆ According to legend, three lamps were hidden away on Maundy Thursday and kept alight until Holy Saturday. Honor this custom by having candlelight devotions every night from Maundy Thursday until Holy Saturday.

◆ Remembering that Jesus and his disciples celebrated the Passover seder, on Maundy Thursday have a seder meal of your own. Serve the traditional foods— matzoh (unleavened bread), wine (or grape juice), lamb bone, eggs, parsley, bitter herbs, and haroseth (cinnamon, apples, and nuts). Check your church library for a book detailing the seder meal. One resource available is *Passover Seder: Ritual and Menu for an Observance by Christians*, by Barbara Balzac Thompson (Augsburg, 1984).

♦   Attend a Maundy Thursday communion service.

♦   On Good Friday, follow the tradition of making a pilgrimage. Take a walk together. Visit a local park. Visit the grave of a friend or relative. While there, read the story of the crucifixion.

♦   Make hot cross buns on Good Friday. The hot cross bun is apparently an old pagan tradition which Christians took over and made their own by adding a cross to the top of the buns. To save time, make hot cross buns by using canned, refrigerated rolls or biscuits from the grocery store. Bake according to directions on the can. Remove from oven. For a dozen buns, apply a glaze made of:

> 1 pound confectioner's sugar (powdered sugar) minus 1 cup of sugar reserved for later use
> enough milk to make the glaze the consistency of chocolate syrup
> ½ cup raisins

Pour the glaze over the buns and put them back in the oven for a minute or two. Remove the buns and let them cool. Meanwhile, mix the remaining 1 cup of confectioner's sugar with a small amount of milk to form a thick icing. Spread, in the shape of a cross, on the buns.

♦   On Good Friday, remember the hours that Jesus suffered on the cross by having a quiet time from noon

until three o'clock. Read Bible accounts of the crucifixion or attend a Good Friday service.

♦ Check out records or tapes of traditional Easter
music from the library. Possibilities include the *St. John
Passion* and the *St. Matthew Passion* by J. S. Bach and
the *Resurrection Symphony* by Mahler.

♦ On Holy Saturday, hold a family worship empha-
sizing the Easter message of salvation, or attend an
Easter vigil at your church.

♦ On Holy Saturday, make an Easter cake in the
shape of a cross to use for your dessert on Easter. Use
a 9″ x 13″ cake pan and cut into the shape of a cross
as shown below. Frost with yellow or white icing and
decorate it with silk or real flowers.

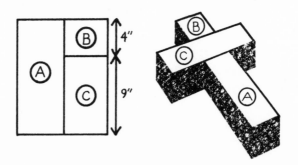

FOUR

EASTER

Beyond the Easter Bunny

Ask most children, and they'll tell you that Easter is the day when the Easter bunny comes. It's fun for children to hunt for eggs and find baskets. But as Christians, we look beyond the bunny to the true meaning of Easter.

"So in Christ all will be made alive," the Bible says. That message is the heart of Easter as we celebrate the great victory, Christ's resurrection. Let's look beyond the new clothes, chocolate eggs, jellybeans, and the Easter bunny. Let's keep the spirit of Easter alive in our celebrations today.

♦ Decorate an artificial tree or a branch which you bring from outside with paper Easter symbols. The following are some of the traditional symbols of Easter:

An empty cross—a symbol of Jesus' death and resurrection.

A donkey—Jesus rode into Jerusalem on Palm Sunday on a donkey.

A robin—its red breast reminds us of the blood Jesus spilled on the cross.

A butterfly—it appears from a dead-looking cocoon, reminding us of the resurrection.

An egg—symbol of new life.

A lion—according to ancient legend, lions were born dead and only brought to life three days later by their mothers—resemblance to Easter story makes the lion a symbol of Easter.

A rabbit—symbol of new life.

A whale or large fish—symbol of the story of Jonah, which some believe is a prophecy of Jesus' death and resurrection.

♦ Send Easter cards to people who are homebound or living in nursing homes. You might deliver them in person and sing a few Easter carols at the same time.

♦ If you plan to buy new Easter outfits for you and your children, buy them at a secondhand store and give the money you save to church or charity.

♦ Make your own Easter candy. Check your cookbook for recipes. Or, make cookies in the shape of eggs and decorate them with colored frosting.

♦ Decorate Easter eggs with watercolor markers, or paint them with acrylic paints. Explain to your children that eggs remind us of new life, and Jesus brought all of us new life when he died and rose again.

◆ Make quick and simple Easter baskets:
Recycle plastic mesh berry baskets from the grocery store. Weave ribbon in and out and fill with Easter grass and a small amount of candy.
Cut a cardboard half-gallon milk carton in half and cover with wrapping paper. Add a pipe cleaner handle and fill with Easter goodies.
Turn an old shoe box into an Easter basket by covering it with paper and filling it with Easter grass and candy.
Give a toy dump truck as a present. Make an Easter nest in the back of the truck.
Start the custom of making an Easter basket in a child's shoe. Children will wake up to find their shoes filled with treats.
Make an Easter nest in your child's cereal bowl and put it at his or her place at the table.

◆ Rise early on Easter morning and decorate your home, rather than putting up decorations during Lent.

◆ Have your own Easter sunrise service at a local park. As the sun rises, sing Easter hymns of praise.

◆ Rent a video which dramatizes the life of Jesus. This is a good Easter afternoon activity or something to do during Holy Week as you prepare for Easter.

◆ If the weather is nice on Easter day, go for a bike ride or have a picnic.

◆ Have a traditional Easter breakfast of eggs before or after church. Or, attend your church's Easter breakfast, if you have one.

♦ Give kites as Easter presents and go kite flying.

♦ Ask each family member to learn an Easter poem or hymn or a scripture passage, such as Psalm 150, and recite it at Easter dinner. Before eating, read the resurrection account from one of the Gospels.

♦ Celebrate new life by spending Easter afternoon preparing for spring planting. If Easter is early, you can spend the day planting seeds in small containers that can be transplanted into the garden later on. Or, sit down with a garden supply catalog and choose plants and seeds that would beautify your yard and nourish your body in the months ahead.

FIVE

MOTHER'S DAY AND FATHER'S DAY

Honor Your Father and Mother

Mother's Day and Father's Day call for a different focus than most holidays. What's important here is that the holiday be meaningful to the parent being honored. Some fathers are thrilled with breakfast in bed. Some aren't. Some mothers love to receive flowers. Others don't. Knowing your mother or father, perceiving how he or she would like to be remembered on this day, is an important aspect of honoring your parent.

♦ Before Mother's or Father's Day, have all the children of the family write about their favorite memories of the parent of honor. Assemble these memoirs into a scrapbook.

♦ List qualities of your mother or father for which you are thankful. Tell or write about these qualities to your parent.

♦ At dinner, offer a special prayer of thanks for your mother and father.

♦ Instead of flowers, give a subscription to a gardening magazine.

♦ Give a donation to a charity of your mother or father's choice.

♦ Give a membership to a fitness center or Y.

♦ Give your mother or father the promise of an outing together. If you're an adult now, you might plan to do something you and your parent enjoyed together when you were a child.

♦ Carry on the tradition of wearing flowers on Mother's Day to honor your mother. Traditionally, each person was supposed to wear a pink carnation if his or her mother was alive and a white carnation if mother was dead. In South Carolina, where I grew up, we wore red or white roses. A big honor on Mother's Day was to have the job of cutting roses for the whole family from our rose bush.

♦ Adopt the French custom of baking and decorating a Mother's Day cake for your mother and serving it at the end of a family meal. You might do the same for your father on Father's Day.

34

♦   In England, Mothering Sunday is a day to honor both your mother church and your own mother. In the past, young people working away from home visited their mothers and the churches where they were baptized on Mothering Sunday. It was customary for the young people to do all their mothers' housework on this day and present her with a plum cake. Adopt some of these Mothering Sunday customs:

Visit, call, or write your mother.
Take your mother a cake.
Visit your home church.
Make a donation to your home church.

♦   Have an art show in which participants enter drawings or paintings of their mothers or fathers.

♦   On Mother's Day or Father's Day discuss the problems which some mothers and fathers face—poverty, homelessness, shortage of quality child care, drug addiction. Decide several ways that you can work together to help mothers or fathers facing these problems.

♦   On Mother's or Father's Day, remember those mothers and fathers who spend these days in prison or who are homeless. Contact a homeless shelter or correctional facility and offer to donate something which would be of use to the mothers and fathers who live in these facilities.

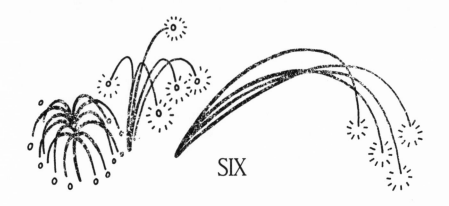

SIX

INDEPENDENCE DAY/CANADA DAY

Celebrating Freedom

Although national independence days aren't religious holidays, they are important days to remember and celebrate. We should not forget that religious freedom was one of our ancestors' primary goals in coming to a new country. Thomas Jefferson wrote, "Let the annual return of this day refresh our recollections of these rights and our undiminished devotion to them." Let's celebrate our independence days in this spirit.

♦ Have a breakfast picnic in the park before the crowds come. Read Bible verses about liberty, for example, Lev. 25:10; Ps. 119:45; John 8:32; Rom. 8:21; 1 Cor. 7:22; Gal. 5:1; 1 Peter 2:15-16.

♦ Younger children would enjoy a family parade around the neighborhood, possibly on bicycles decorated with crepe paper streamers.

+ Visit a nursing home and talk to residents about their memories of Independence Day or Canada Day.

+ Bring back the old custom of having an older child read aloud from the Declaration of Independence.

+ Ask everyone in the group to prepare a speech or memorize poetry in honor of Independence Day or Canada Day.

+ Read aloud from the writings of people who struggled for freedom in their lives, such as Martin Luther, Thomas Jefferson, Gandhi, or Martin Luther King Jr.

+ Spend a quiet independence day by taking a walking tour of churches in your community. Talk about the religious freedom which allows such diversity.

+ On the first anniversary of the Fourth of July, many families lit candles in their windows in honor of Independence Day. Adopt this custom in your family.

+ Join the people of Wisconsin and Arizona by honoring Native Americans on Independence Day. Plan an afternoon of games and activities that were part of Native American culture, such as the following:
   dodgeball
   kickball
   tug-of-war
   breath-holding contests

wrestling
canoeing

♦ During your family devotions, pray for national and local leaders. Pray also for those who struggle for liberty today. Thank God for the freedoms we enjoy.

SEVEN

HALLOWEEN

Is There a Christian Way to Celebrate the Day?

A friend of mine does not celebrate Halloween because she believes it's a pagan holiday. She won't allow her children to trick or treat and doesn't hand out candy to the neighborhood kids.

Is she right? It's true that Halloween does have pagan roots. And it is the night of black magic, witchcraft, and demons. For this reason, perhaps we shouldn't play up the holiday. But the celebration of October 31 can be tied to a Christian celebration. It is the eve of All Saints' Day, the day set aside by the Christian church to remember those who now dwell with the Lord.

If you believe as my friend does, you may wish to skip this chapter. But I suggest that we turn Halloween around and make it a positive celebration, keeping in mind that though there is evil in the world, Christ conquers all evil.

◆ If you choose to trick or treat, limit the number of houses your children visit. Visit only friends rather than every house in the neighborhood. One mother set the rule, "When the bottom of the bag is covered, it's time to go home."

◆ Instead of trick or treating, do something together as a family. You might:
    play games
    eat popcorn and drink apple cider
    bob for apples
    go to a movie or stay home and rent a video
    go skating or bowling

◆ Host an "All Hallow's Eve" party and invite friends to come dressed as their favorite saint from the past, with a saint being any good person whom they admire. Have everyone share stories about their designated saint.

◆ Invite a few friends to come to a costume party. They must wear costumes made using only newspapers, tape, and felt-tipped markers.

◆ Hold a hunt for the missing saint. Give clues leading to the hiding place of the saint, a dummy made by stuffing some old clothes. Pin a name tag to the saint. The object of this game is for the players to discover the saint's identity and hiding place and be the first person to whisper it to the game leader.
    Give each player an initial clue at the beginning of the hunt. Each clue leads to another clue. (Hint: Give each player a different first clue. That way they will

be finding subsequent clues at different times.) Possible clues could include:

It's the only place in the house where time still ticks away. (*On the back of a windup alarm clock.*)

Without me, the porch would fall in. (*On one of the columns on a porch.*)

A person could sit and watch TV and never notice I'm here. (*Under the armrest of a chair in the family room.*)

You might also look here for something to eat. (*In the refrigerator.*)

The only place with a dirt floor. (*In the cellar.*)

My title is *Robinson Crusoe.* (*In the bookcase.*)

♦ Invite friends to a potluck dinner, where everything brought is to contain apples or pumpkin.

♦ If you can find an inexpensive source of pumpkins, have a pumpkin-decorating contest. Carve or decorate with markers or acrylic paint.

♦ If you choose to trick or treat, make homemade costumes. Let your children paint their faces with face crayons. Limit costumes to non-scary creations.

♦ Make caramel apples together, using the recipe on the caramels package.

♦ Turn out the lights and play Sardines. One person hides and everybody hunts for him or her. When they find the person, they stay there until everybody joins them.

♦ Play hide-and-seek in the dark. Provide the person who is "it" with a flashlight. If that person catches someone with the flashlight beam, he or she joins "it" in the search for others.

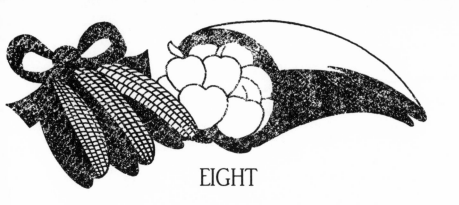

EIGHT

THANKSGIVING

Feast but Do Not Forget to Thank

We all enjoy getting together with family and sharing a special meal at Thanksgiving. Still, many of us are uncomfortable with the notion of gathering together to gorge ourselves on more food than we want or need. We also remember that many people will not have any meal on this day, much less a feast. We want to celebrate Thanksgiving in a responsible manner. We want to celebrate Thanksgiving with thankful hearts. It *is* possible.

♦ Attend your church's or community's Thanksgiving service as a family. If there are no services on Thanksgiving Day, hold a family service of prayer and Thanksgiving.

◆ Instead of making excessive amounts of food, keep your Thanksgiving dinner to normal dinnertime proportions. Don't force second helpings.

◆ Plan several meatless meals for the week before Thanksgiving.

◆ Donate money to an organization that serves a free Thanksgiving Day meal or volunteer to serve such a meal.

◆ Donate money to an organization that helps to fight world hunger. Take food items to your local food pantry.

◆ Invite someone who may be alone to share your meal with you.

◆ Send homemade Thanksgiving cards to people who are homebound or living in nursing homes.

◆ Study books about the causes of world hunger such as *Food First* by Frances Moore Lappé and Joseph Collins.

◆ Set an extra place at your table to remind family members of those who are without food. Include those people in your Thanksgiving prayer.

◆ Read aloud the story of the first Thanksgiving before you eat your meal. Or, act it out for afternoon entertainment.

♦ As you pray before your meal, invite each person to offer individual prayers of thanks.

♦ Put a cornucopia ("horn of plenty") on your table and invite family members to fill it with items that represent how you have been blessed. You might include foods and more commercial symbols like cassette tapes, clothing accessories, photos of items and people, etc.

♦ Take the burden off the cook not by going out to eat but by offering to help. Even small children can set the table. The greatest help anyone can offer is to wash the dishes.

♦ Start the tradition of the "Blessings Basket." At the conclusion of the Thanksgiving meal, set a large basket in the middle of the table. From then on until Christmas, each day add to the basket food and gifts for a needy family.

♦ Read the Bible together at mealtime and before bed, remembering that this was a Pilgrim custom.

♦ Use Thanksgiving afternoon as a time to plan for Advent and Christmas.

♦ If you're having a large family get-together with many small children, take turns watching the children so that one or two people don't get stuck with the burden. Offer to get the kids out of the house for a while by taking them to the park. This especially helps at cleanup time.

♦ Instead of turning on the football game, go outside and play something yourself. Or, take a long walk after dinner.

♦ Use Thanksgiving as a time to honor Native Americans. Read aloud Native American folktales. Talk about contributions that Native Americans have made to our culture.

♦ Discuss the Native American tradition of using symbols to show something about yourself. Have each family member draw and explain symbols about himself or herself. For instance, one person might draw a fire to represent a bad temper and a pair of outstretched hands to represent a desire to forgive and be forgiven. You might wish to have everyone draw their symbols on paper placemats and use them at Thanksgiving dinner.

♦ Share in the Native American respect for God's creation by spending time outdoors on Thanksgiving. If the weather is mild, you might even have a Thanksgiving picnic.

♦ As Thanksgiving approaches, visit the library together and learn about Native Americans who once lived in your area. Use the information you find to prepare posters and drawings of these Native Americans. Display them during the Thanksgiving season.

♦ On the day after Thanksgiving, visit a museum with displays depicting Native American life.

NINE

CHRISTMAS

Remember the Reason for the Season

Some people would claim that keeping the Christmas season sane yet satisfying is impossible in this day of Christmas overkill. People complain of having too many parties to attend, too many sweets to eat, too many presents to buy. Sometimes it sounds as if these people wish Christmas would go away and leave them alone. The key to enjoying Christmas lies in getting back to the true reason for celebrating in the first place: the birth of our Savior, Jesus. Once that is given its priority status, we can begin to look at Christmas and the preparation for it in an entirely new way. We can welcome Christmas! Try the suggestions in this chapter for making the Christmas season a time to enjoy rather than wish away.

One way to keep from getting caught up in the Christmas frenzy is to celebrate Advent, the season of anticipation and preparation. Advent begins four Sundays before Christmas Day and concludes on Christmas Eve.

♦ Make or purchase an Advent wreath. Have daily Advent devotions with your family as you light the Advent candles. Many Advent devotion booklets are available for your use. Check with your church or local Christian bookstore.

♦ Instead of an Advent wreath, consider decorating a Jesse Tree. Named for Jesse, the father of King David, the tree helps us remember the biblical people who helped prepare the world for the birth of Jesus. Decorate a tree branch with homemade symbols representing people in the Bible, such as Abraham and Sarah, David, John the Baptist, and others. Add one symbol a day until Christmas. A resource that describes the Jesse Tree is *Jesse Tree Devotions* by Marilyn S. Breckenridge (Augsburg, 1985).

♦ Decorate your Christmas tree with homemade decorations such as paper chains, bread dough ornaments, cookies, and popcorn strings. Many people don't realize that you can keep popcorn strings for years. Store them in a plastic bag and keep with your other decorations. We've had some of ours for eight years now.

♦ Decorate your tree over a series of evenings. Put the lights on one night, then add ornaments, garland, etc., on successive evenings. Hold your devotions around the tree.

♦ Send homemade cards. Recycle old gift wrap by cutting out holiday shapes from it and gluing on construction paper cards. Let children draw Christmas scenes on blank cards.

♦ Set up your Nativity scene beneath your Christmas tree. You might add one figure each day for several days, and save the baby Jesus figure until Christmas Eve.

♦ Celebrate St. Nicholas Day (December 6). St. Nicholas was a priest who lived in Asia Minor during the fourth century A.D. According to legend, he furnished dowries for three poor girls whose father couldn't afford to pay them. He did this at night by throwing sacks of coins into the girls' bedrooms. This is how the custom of nighttime visits from St. Nicholas originated. In some countries, children still receive presents on St. Nicholas Day rather than at Christmas. Why not make St. Nicholas Day a part of your Advent by trying some of the following activities?

Exchange small gifts at breakfast on St. Nicholas Day.

Have someone dress as St. Nicholas, with a long white robe and sack, and visit the family after supper. St. Nicholas might ask the children about their plans for Advent and pull cookies out of his bag for everyone.

Make St. Nicholas Day a time for exchanging gifts that can be used during Advent. For instance:

a book about Christmas

construction paper and crayons for making Christmas cards

a Christmas decoration

ingredients for making a special Christmas cookie recipe
Christmas stamps
Christmas napkins
a tape of Christmas music

♦ Remember our animal friends at Christmas. Take Christmas presents of food to your local animal shelter or make a donation of money.

♦ Give the birds a Christmas present. Make simple bird feeders using pinecones. Spread peanut butter over the pinecones and roll them in bird seed. String the feeders from tree branches. Continue to feed the birds throughout the winter.

♦ Do your Christmas shopping early and then stay away from the stores. Or wait until closer to Christmas to shop, but do it all in one day. Make a special occasion out of the day.

♦ Consider buying one gift for the family rather than individual gifts.

♦ Limit the number of gifts you buy to one per person, or set a dollar amount limit for each gift.

♦ Make your gifts this year. Or, donate money to charitable organizations on behalf of the people on your gift list.

♦ Take the emphasis off gifts by not placing them under the tree. Bring them out right before you open them instead.

♦ Place Christmas books under the tree and set aside time each day to read and reflect on the wonder of Jesus' birth.

♦ Keep holiday shopping simple. Most of us have a tendency to buy more than what's necessary to make our family happy.

♦ Consider drawing names among extended family members for gift giving.

♦ Don't ask children to make a Christmas list. This usually leads them to ask for more presents than they would have otherwise.

♦ Make an audiotape to send to family and friends you won't see at Christmas. It's quicker than writing a long letter. You can talk into the tape recorder while you're doing something else like making Christmas cookies.

♦ Send a videotape of the family to family members you won't see at Christmas.

♦ Baking cookies is for most people a Christmas ritual, but bake only one or two kinds instead of a dozen. Organize a cookie exchange with friends and neighbors.

♦ At Christmas, donate a book to your local library.

♦ As you shop, pick up a toy for your local Toys for Tots or Santa Anonymous campaign.

♦ Call a homeless shelter or shelter for abused women and ask if you may bring Christmas gifts for the residents.

♦ Make personalized calendars as Christmas gifts for family members. Cut out pictures of members of the family and paste them on the dates of their birthdays. Mark special days throughout the year.

♦ Celebrate the season with nightly candlelight dinners. Play Christmas carols on the stereo.

♦ Adopt a Mexican custom and make a Christmas piñata. There are books at the library to show you how. If you don't have time to make a traditional piñata (it takes about two hours over a two-day period), try making this quick piñata. Decorate a large paper bag using markers. Fill the bag with candy. Tie it at the top with string. Suspend the bag from a broomstick or hang it in a doorway. Blindfold children and let them take turns trying to break it with a plastic baseball bat.

♦ Mexican families reenact the drama of Mary and Joseph's search for a room at the inn during the days before Christmas. Make this ritual, called La Posada, a part of your Advent celebration. Choose a night during Advent to dramatize La Posada with another family. Walk or drive to their home. Carry with you your nativity set figures. Knock on the door. When they answer, you say, "Is there room in the inn?", explaining that Mary must have a place to bear her child. At first, the host family says there is no room in the inn, but after being asked several times, they let the visitors come inside their home. The host family finds a place of honor for the nativity set. Everyone celebrates with food and a piñata for the children.

♦   Adopt this Polish custom at your Christmas dinner: Have one person ask each of the others a question about the Christmas story. Each person who answers correctly receives a small gift from the magi.

TEN

BIRTHDAYS

Celebrate the Day without the Hassle

The newest trend in birthday parties is to hold them at fast-food restaurants. Several parents have defended this practice, saying, "It's cheaper than having the party at home." This can be true, depending on how elaborate your party plans are. But I see parties at fast-food places as more of an advertisement for the restaurant than a birthday celebration. Most of all, what I dislike about these fast-food birthday celebrations is the message behind them: "Don't be bothered with giving your child a birthday party. We can do it as well or even better."

Don't be fooled. The simplest birthday celebration you plan will be ten times better than what any fast-food place has to offer. And it need not involve a lot of time. The following are some easy ways to celebrate birthdays at home.

♦   Cook hamburgers or hotdogs at a local park and play at the playground. Easier yet, pack sack lunches to take along. Peanut butter and jelly are perennial favorites.

♦   Go on a family outing to a museum or historical site.

♦   Serve the birthday person breakfast in bed.

♦   Fix the birthday person's favorite dinner. Instead of a cake, stick a candle in a scoop of ice cream.

♦   According to an old German custom, families decorate a small tree in honor of the birthday person and leave his or her presents under it.

♦   Follow the Dutch tradition of keeping a birthday calendar with the birthdates of family members written on it.

♦   Celebrate birthdays as they do in Iran by hiding the birthday person's gifts and having him or her hunt for them.

♦   After the birthday person blows out the candles and makes a wish, let others tell what they wish for the birthday person.

♦   A mother of grown children said that she misses her children most on their birthdays. Try to visit your parents on your birthday, or at least call them.

♦ Make the birthday person a basketful of things to enjoy on the special day. You might include some of the following:

a paperback book

hot chocolate, gourmet coffee, or an assortment of tea bags

bubblebath

a cassette tape of favorite music or a book by his or her favorite author

ingredients for a special dinner and a promise to cook it

samples of favorite treats such as nuts or chocolates

Birthday Party Ideas

If you decide to have a party for a child, keep it small and simple. A good rule to keep in mind is to invite one guest for each of the child's years. For example, a three-year-old would have three guests. Keep the party short (no more than an hour).

♦ Have a sledding party for a winter birthday.

♦ If you have a computer, have a computer games party.

♦ Have a building party using all your Legos, blocks, Tinkertoys, and any other building toys.

♦ If you're a member of the Y or other indoor pool, have a swimming party in the wintertime.

♦ Have a baseball party where the children play baseball as their main activity.

♦ Hold a scavenger hunt. Possible items to find are:

a penny	an acorn
a feather	a pinecone
a piece of gravel	a candy bar wrapper
a receipt from a grocery store	a gum wrapper
a paper cup	a leaf

♦ For a winter party, have a magazine scavenger hunt. Ask children to look for objects commonly found in magazines. They can cut out pictures of objects on the list.

♦ For a winter birthday in a cold climate, invite children to come and build a huge snow fort. Serve cake and hot chocolate afterwards.

♦ For a summer birthday, plan a water games party. Ask the children to bring their swimming suits. Have a water balloon battle, play water balloon volleyball, and squirt each other with the hose.

♦ Let the children make paper airplanes and fly them instead of playing competitive games.

♦ Have your child invite one or two friends and take them tubing in a nearby shallow creek, or visit a water slide park. Return to your house for cake and ice cream.

♦ Arrange to take the kids on a tour of the police or fire station.

♦ Have a breakfast birthday party. Put candles in the pancakes. This is great for sleepovers.

♦ Let the birthday child invite one friend to a concert, movie, or museum.

♦ Play non-competitive games such as the following:
  Make an audiotape of various sounds such as water running, a door slamming, hammering, a vacuum cleaner, an alarm clock. Let the children identify the sounds.
  Make an audiotape of songs they would know or play them on a musical instrument. Ask them to identify the songs.
  Let the children play with clay or Playdough.
  Let the children paint.
  Give each child a bowl of watered-down dishwashing detergent. Give each a wand you've made ahead of time using one pipe cleaner for the stem and fastening a circle made of two pipe cleaners to the stem. Let the children go outside and blow bubbles.

♦ Have a playground party. Meet at a local playground. The playground equipment will provide the entertainment.

Birthday Party Refreshment Ideas

Keep it simple, especially for younger children. Keep the portions small. Cake, ice cream, and juice or milk is plenty.

♦ Instead of cake, let the children decorate their own cupcakes with ready-to-serve frosting and candy decorations.

♦ Let older children make their own sundaes.

♦ Older children can make pizzas using English muffins, pizza sauce, and cheese.

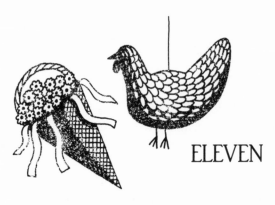

ELEVEN

OTHER DAYS TO CELEBRATE

Adopt a Holiday

There are many holidays we don't usually celebrate. In some instances, these may be legal holidays around which we haven't yet developed our own traditions or church holidays that typically aren't celebrated in the home. Consider adopting some of these special days to enrich your family life.

Boxing Day

This English holiday, which falls on the day after Christmas, was traditionally the day on which the lord of the manor took presents to his servants. Later, it became a day to take boxes of food to the needy. Observe Boxing Day by gathering a box of food for your local food pantry.

Epiphany

Epiphany, on January 6, commemorates the day the Wise Men arrived with gifts for the baby Jesus. Although churches observe Epiphany, families in our country rarely celebrate it. Here are a few traditional customs we can take for our own and a few new ones we might choose to adopt.

♦ Epiphany is the traditional time for taking down the Christmas tree. This is often a lonely chore done by one person. Why not make taking the ornaments off the tree a family ritual? If you usually have a star atop your tree, make it the final thing to remove. Play Christmas music for the last time of the season. Have refreshments and share your memories of the season just passed.

♦ Attend an Epiphany service, if your church is holding one. If not, observe Epiphany in your own family worship. Read the story of the Wise Men from Matthew 2:1-12. Sing an Epiphany hymn or the familiar carol, "We Three Kings of Orient Are." Pray together, thanking God for the precious gift of Jesus.

♦ Exchange small presents in honor of the Wise Men.

♦ Check out from your library the book, *The Legend of Old Befana,* by Tomie dePaola and read aloud as a bedtime story. The book is an illustrated retelling of an Italian folktale about a peasant woman who went seeking the Christ child.

♦ Follow the Mexican custom of writing letters to the Wise Men on Epiphany. Put the emphasis on the spiritual gifts you wish for on this day.

♦ Bake an Epiphany cake using a cake mix. According to an old custom popular in many countries, a bean is slipped into the cake batter. Whoever finds the bean in his or her slice of cake becomes the guest of honor at the Epiphany celebration.

Martin Luther King Jr. Day

This national holiday in the United States falls on the Monday nearest the birthday of Martin Luther King Jr., January 15th. On this day we honor the faith, determination, and courage of this civil rights leader.

♦ Attend a church service held in honor of Martin Luther King Jr.

♦ Read aloud from a book about Martin Luther King Jr. or read some of his speeches like the "I Have a Dream" speech.

♦ Discuss your own dreams for the world community.

♦ Have a candlelight dinner in honor of Martin Luther King Jr. and talk about his life.

♦ Talk about instances of injustice and prejudice you have observed or experienced. (Children deal with

these issues daily on the playground and in the class-
room.) Determine ways you might deal with such sit-
uations in the future. Pray for wisdom and strength to
stand up for what is good and just.

Candlemas

Candlemas, on February 2, honors the visit Mary,
Joseph, and Jesus made to the temple 40 days after
Christmas. It is a tradition to light candles on this day
as a symbol that Christ is the light of the world. In
your own family, you might light candles at the dinner
table to commemorate this occasion. Read aloud the
story of Simeon and Anna from Luke 2:22-38.

Chinese New Year

Focus on other cultures by holding a celebration on
the Chinese New Year, which occurs some time be-
tween January 21 and February 19. Have a special
family dinner featuring foods from China. According
to Chinese tradition, children receive red envelopes
holding paper money. You might adapt this custom by
having everyone write wishes for other family members
and stuff them into envelopes. Each person then receives an envelope full of good wishes for the new year.

World Day of Prayer

The first Friday in Lent is the World Day of Prayer.
On this day, Christians all over the world gather to
pray together. The focus is on mutual understanding

and world peace. Women have traditionally played an important role in the World Day of Prayer. Mark this day on your calendar and set it aside as a special time to offer your prayers for peace and unity. Attend a World Day of Prayer service in your community or hold your own family prayer service.

May Day

On May 1st we celebrate springtime. May Day is traditionally a time of surprise gifts. Make May baskets for neighbors by filling empty fruit containers with grass, flowers, and a small amount of candy. Leave the baskets on neighbors' porches. Or, take a walk through your neighborhood on May Day and clean up any trash you find.

Arbor Day

Arbor Day is the time set aside for planting trees. There is no set date for Arbor Day. Most states have designated as Arbor Day some time when the weather is suitable for planting trees. Planting trees has been part of religious celebrations in many cultures. Make Arbor Day a part of your celebration of God's creation.

◆ Plant a tree to honor the birth of a child.

◆ Borrow customs from the Jewish festival, the New Year of the Trees. Talk about ways trees help us. Make and display posters showing how trees help us. Offer to buy a tree for your church or school. Have a party in honor of trees. Serve only food that came from trees such as nuts, carob, apples, peaches, cherries, figs, and dates.

Ascension Day

This Thursday, 40 days after Easter, honors the day when Jesus ascended into heaven. Mark the day by flying kites and reading Bible passages about the ascension (Mark 16:19-20; Luke 24:44-53; Acts 1:4-11). Or, borrow the old English custom of decorating with flowers on Ascension Day.

Pentecost

Pentecost falls 50 days after Easter. Christians remember the day as the birthday of the church, the day the Holy Spirit came to the disciples.

◆   Red is the traditional color for Pentecost Sunday. Wear red in honor of the day.

◆   Read the Pentecost story from Acts 20.

◆   According to legend, any wish you make at sunrise on Pentecost will come true. Get up early on the day of Pentecost, and make a spiritual wish for your family.

Memorial Day

In the United States, Memorial Day is observed on the last Monday in May. Originally the day set aside to decorate the graves of soldiers, it has become just a long weekend holiday for most people. A good way to recall the true meaning of the day is by visiting your local cemetery and decorating the graves of all loved ones. Many communities also hold special Memorial programs. Keeping in mind the many people who have died in war, pray that peace might prevail today.

Water Festival

In Thailand, people celebrate God's gift of water with a water festival. On a hot summer day, have your own water festival. Drink ice water, go swimming, squirt each other with water guns. Talk about why water is vital in our lives. You might discuss the role water plays in baptism.

Labor Day

This legal holiday in the United States falls on the first Monday in September, traditionally signaling the end of summer vacation. Observe the work-related theme of the day by talking about what you do for a living. Think about ways you can serve God in your place of work.

♦ Children enjoy dreaming about what they want to do "when they grow up." Encourage small children to draw pictures of their favorite occupation. Older children can read a book from the library on a chosen job.

♦ Write thank-you notes to people who may work for you, to coworkers, or to those for whom you work.

Harvest Celebration

Keep an African tradition by holding a corn roast to celebrate the harvest.

Mexican-Style Fiestas

Mexicans hold frequent fiestas to honor saints. Choose dates to honor people who have been important in your life. You might want to honor a relative who has meant a lot to your family or a public figure whom you admire.

Kristallnacht—November 9th

On this night in 1938, the Nazis went on a rampage against the Jews in Germany, killing and injuring many, wrecking synagogues, and destroying property. As Christians we can remember this tragic day by holding a silent candlelight service. Or, read Bible passages about tolerance (Prov. 11:12; Matt. 5:43-44; Matt. 7:1; Acts 10:28; 1 Cor. 13:4-7; Titus 3:2) and forgiveness (Prov. 24:17, 28; Prov. 25:21; Matt. 6:14; Mark 11:25; Col. 3:12-13).

Sabbath

According to the Bible, we should "remember the Sabbath day, to keep it holy." As Christians, we choose to remember the "Sabbath" on Sunday. Like other holidays, Sunday can be a day of rituals.

♦   Attend church together as a family.

♦   Adopt some customs from the Jewish people. On Saturday, bake a special bread to eat on the Sabbath. Use your best tablecloth, china, and silverware for a candlelight Sabbath meal.

♦   Establish a Sunday ritual. When I was growing up, visiting my grandparents on Sunday afternoon was our ritual. Now our ritual is ordering pizza.

♦   Try to make no commitment outside the family on Sunday.

♦   Refrain from making Sunday just another day. Try not to do your yardwork or housecleaning on Sunday. Establish some special routines that set Sunday apart from the rest of the week.

♦   Make the English custom of afternoon tea part of your Sabbath. Make tea, coffee, or hot chocolate and serve it along with sandwiches, warm breads, muffins, cookies, or cakes.

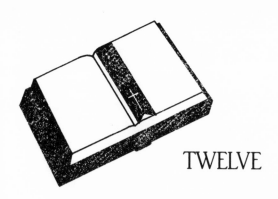

TWELVE

FAMILY WORSHIP AND DEVOTIONS

Keeping Christ in Your Holidays

Holding family devotions or worship services is an ideal way to put meaning back into your holidays. By doing so, we keep Christ from being shoved aside in favor of the Easter bunny, Santa Claus, parades, or bowl games. A brief family worship goes a long way toward reminding us why we are celebrating each holiday.

Consider also holding daily family devotions using one of the devotional guides often available at churches. Perhaps your problem is finding the time. You might hold your family devotions as you gather around the supper table or after you finish the evening meal. Another possibility is to hold your devotions as you tuck a child into bed.

This chapter contains prayers, litanies, and devotionals for some of the holidays in this book. Let these worship suggestions be a stepping-off point for your family. Personalize them in ways that are meaningful to you.

New Year's Eve Litany

Lord, be with us as we wait for this new year to begin.

MY SOUL WAITS FOR THE LORD MORE THAN WATCHMEN WAIT FOR THE MORNING.

Know our hopes for this coming year.

IT IS GOOD THAT WE SHOULD BOTH HOPE AND QUIETLY WAIT FOR THE SALVATION OF THE LORD.

We have no idea what this new year may bring. Help us have the faith to meet what comes.

FAITH IS BEING SURE OF WHAT WE HOPE FOR AND CERTAIN OF WHAT WE DO NOT SEE.

Help us to do your will by serving others in the coming year.

WE ARE GOD'S FELLOW WORKERS.

Give us courage.

ENABLE US TO SERVE THE LORD WITHOUT FEAR, IN HOLINESS AND RIGHTEOUSNESS BEFORE THE LORD ALL THE DAYS OF OUR LIVES.

Help us to be the best people we can be during this new year.

HELP US LIVE LIVES WORTHY OF THE LORD, PLEASING GOD IN EVERY WAY, DOING

GOOD WORK, AND GROWING IN OUR
KNOWLEDGE OF GOD.

Epiphany Family Devotion

Read Matthew 2:1-12

We all know the story of the Wise Men who brought
gifts to the baby Jesus. According to one legend, there
was a meaning behind each of the gifts the Wise Men
brought. One brought gold to show that Jesus was King.
Another brought incense, used in religious ceremonies,
to show that Jesus was from God. The third brought
myrrh, used in burial, to symbolize the baby's humanity.
But the legend does not stop with these gifts from
the Wise Men. Jesus, it says, exchanged gifts with each
of them. In exchange for the gold, he gave spiritual
wealth. For the incense, he offered faith. For the
myrrh, he gave truth and humility. We will be as blessed
as the Wise Men if we can receive these spiritual gifts
from Christ on this Epiphany.

Prayer: Dear God, help us open our hearts to the
spiritual wealth which is ours through Christ. We value
these gifts of faith, truth, and humility above all others.
We thank you in Jesus' name. Amen.

Lenten Litany for Shrove Tuesday (Based on Matthew 4:1-11)

We face many temptations in our day-to-day lives that
lead us from your way, Lord.

JESUS WAS LED BY THE SPIRIT INTO THE DE-
SERT TO BE TEMPTED BY THE DEVIL.

Every way we turn, people are saying that the way of
the Lord is foolish. What's important is having the
right things and as much of them as we can get.

JESUS SAID, "IT IS WRITTEN. MAN DOES NOT
LIVE BY BREAD ALONE, BUT ON EVERY
WORD THAT COMES FROM THE MOUTH OF
GOD."

But we want to be important people, too, Lord. We
want others to look at us and say, "That's *somebody.*"
You don't want me to be a nobody. I know that,
Lord.

JESUS SAID, "IT IS ALSO WRITTEN, DO NOT
PUT THE LORD YOUR GOD TO THE TEST."

There's so much I want to have, God. A closet full of
clothes. A new house. A Mercedes in the garage.
Fame. I'd do anything to have it all.

JESUS SAID, "AWAY FROM ME, SATAN. FOR IT
IS WRITTEN: WORSHIP THE LORD YOUR
GOD AND SERVE HIM ONLY."

Prayer for Unity on the World Day of Prayer

How good and pleasant it is when brothers and sisters
live together in unity.

WE WALK TOGETHER.

In our hearts we will not think evil of each other.

WE ARE ALL BROTHERS AND SISTERS TO-
GETHER.

We will carry each other's burdens.

AND FULFILL THE LAW OF CHRIST.

Let there be no divisions among us. Let us be perfectly
united in mind and thought.

LET US LIVE TOGETHER IN PEACE.

Did not one God create us?

WE ARE ALL CHILDREN OF GOD.

There is one body and one spirit, one Lord, one faith,
and one baptism.

THERE IS ONE GOD AND ONE FATHER OF ALL,
WHO IS OVER ALL AND THROUGH ALL AND
IN ALL.

Candlelight Family Devotions for Holy Week

Begin each of your Holy Week devotions in the same
way, by having each person light a candle and read
one of the following verses:

The Lord is my light and salvation.

The unfolding of your words gives light.

The Lord is our everlasting light.

Jesus is the light of the world.

In him was life, and that life was the light of the
world.

The Lord is light, and in him there is no darkness
at all.

Each night during Holy Week read part of the story
of Christ's Passion (Matt. 21:1-11; 26–27; Mark 11:1-
11; 14:12—15:47; Luke 19:28-40; 22–23; or John
12:12-19; 13; 18–19). At the end of each night's reading, put out the candles and sit in darkness for a few
minutes of silent prayer and reflection.

Easter Morning Family Worship

Begin by having each person read or recite one of the following verses:

The Lord is risen!
He is risen indeed!
Sing for joy, O heavens, for the Lord has done this.
Shout aloud, O earth beneath. Burst into song, you
  mountains, you forests, and all your trees.
Our joy is complete.

Next read the story of Easter from the Bible (Matt. 28:1-10; Mark 16:1-20; Luke 24:1-12; or John 20:1-18).

Prayer: God, help us to feel the power of the resurrection in our lives not just today but every day. Help us remember that no matter how deep our gloom, this truth endures—Christ is risen! Amen.

Litany for Arbor Day

O taste and see that the Lord is good. Blessed is the
  one who has faith in him.
WE HAVE FAITH IN THE LORD.
The earth is the Lord's and everything in it.
WE HAVE FAITH IN THE LORD.
He has made everything beautiful in his time.
WE HAVE FAITH IN THE LORD.
Like the tree which grows and strengthens
WE WILL REMAIN TRUE TO THE FAITH.

We have faith in the Lord. The Lord endures forever.

Litany for Independence Day

Lord, hear our thanks for the religious freedom we so
often take for granted.
THANK YOU, LORD.
Help us remember on this day those who fought so
that we could have this freedom.
WE WILL ALWAYS REMEMBER.
Help us avoid becoming complacent and making liberty
an empty word.
HELP US, LORD.
Help us to become devoted champions for the prin-
ciples of liberty for all people, not just in this nation
but in the world.
HELP US, LORD.
Help us remember the responsibilities that our freedom
entails—responsibilities to our nation, to other peo-
ple, and to God.
HELP US, LORD.
Let us remember that we are never truly independent
of you and would never wish to be.
WE REMEMBER, LORD.

Family Thanksgiving Worship

Opening Prayer:
Thank you, God, for all our blessings on this day.
Thank you for this family, for this home, for this food

on our table. Let us never take for granted these bless-ings which you have given us. In the name of Jesus Christ, our Lord. Amen.

Litany of Thanksgiving

You have given us so much. We are truly thankful for all you have provided.

PRAISE THE LORD.

Keep us from becoming addicted to material wealth. It's so easy to want more and more. Keep us from being like the greedy dogs who can never have enough.

HELP US, LORD.

Keep us from being like those rich people who really have nothing.

HELP US, LORD.

On this day of Thanksgiving, let us remember those who are homeless and hungry.

HELP US, LORD.

On this day of Thanksgiving, help us remember those who are weak.

HELP US, LORD.

Give us the strength to defend them.

HELP US, LORD.

As you have shared so many blessings with us, you also share your strength.

WE RECEIVE OUR STRENGTH FROM YOU, LORD.

We are truly blessed.

WE WILL PRAISE YOU FOREVER.

Christmas Devotional Reading

Read Luke 1:26-38

One December my husband, five-year-old son, and I drove toward the Philadelphia airport. The forecast was for snow. Radio announcers advised everybody to go home and stay there. We couldn't.

There was no turning back from what awaited us at the airport. Our new son was arriving on a plane from the Philippines. I thought of Mary and Joseph and their wintertime journey. Conditions weren't the best for them either as they headed toward Bethlehem. Mary was due to give birth any day. Bethlehem was jammed with people. And Mary and Joseph must have been scared to death of what lay ahead of them. They must have wanted to run back home and forget all about what awaited them at Bethlehem. But they couldn't turn back either.

Snow began falling as we arrived at the airport. The plane landed. People crowded around to see the children coming off the plane. First came a quiet baby. Next came a smiling five-year-old who walked right up and took his new father's hand. Then came our son, Michael. He took one look at us and screamed. Mary and Joseph couldn't have been any more worried about the future than I was at that moment.

We finally calmed down Michael with the help of some crackers and a toy truck. That was when a man came up to me and shook my hand.

"You people are beautiful," he said.

Beautiful? I knew that wasn't true. We weren't any more beautiful than he or anybody else.

Neither were Mary and Joseph. Artists have done us a disservice by painting them with beautiful faces and halos over their heads. The truth was, Mary and Joseph wouldn't have made it onto anybody's Most Beautiful People list. Yet God chose for Mary and Joseph, ordinary people, the most important role ever.

Christmas transforms our everyday world into an extraordinary place. We ordinary people can become extraordinary, too—at Christmas and all through the year. That was God's plan for Mary and Joseph, ordinary people. And it is God's plan for us, too.

Prayer: Dear Lord, help us to be open to your plans for us during this Christmas season and throughout the year. Thank you for sending us your Son, Jesus. Amen.